ALLIGATOR & CROCODILE RESCUE

American alligator hides are wheeled away for processing. Thanks to conservation efforts, the species is no longer endangered.

2000 One-quarter of crocs are still critically endangered. Meanwhile, new problems appear in countries where crocodiles are again common. Programs are designed to control crocodiles for public safety, while ensuring their continued survival.

2003 Captive-bred Chinese alligators wearing monitoring devices are released into protected areas, with hopes that more releases will follow.

CROCS & GATORS: WHAT'S THE DIFFERENCE?

Many people use the words crocodile and alligator as though they're talking about the same thing. Sure, they have things in common, but there are also lots of differences. (As one wildlife biologist puts it: "Listing all of them would be like comparing a jaguar with a lion.") And what exactly are caimans and gharials? Here are a few ways to identify crocodilians:

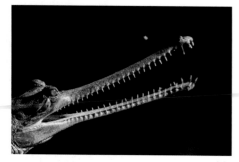

∧ A gharial's snout is perfect for snagging fish.

Look at the shape of the jaw. Alligators and caimans usually have a rounded, U-shaped snout that looks a bit like a garden spade. This broad shape is built for power, and it's capable of cracking open turtles and other hard-shelled invertebrates such as crabs, which are regularly on a gator's menu. Crocodiles tend to have a longer, V-shaped nose. While not as strong, it's good for the wide variety of prey a crocodile might come across. It's easy to spot the gharial by its very thin, pointy nose, which is good for catching fish.

Notice the teeth. The upper jaw of an alligator is wider than the lower jaw, so the bottom teeth are almost completely hidden when the gator's mouth closes. In crocodiles, the upper and lower jaw are about the same width, so the upper and lower teeth interlock when its mouth closes. In a crocodile's closed mouth, look for a large fourth tooth on the lower jaw pointing upward—there's a spot for it to sit comfortably outside the upper jaw, just behind the nostrils.

Look at the small, black spots around the jaws. These spots are believed to allow the reptiles to detect prey by helping help them feel changes in water pressure caused by animal movement. Crocodiles have these receptors covering almost every scale on their bodies, but alligators and caimans have them only around the jaws.

Look at their nostrils. An alligator's nostrils are far apart, with a broad area of skin between them. Crocodiles' nostrils are much closer together.

^ (top) An alligator's bottom teeth are mostly hidden when its mouth is closed.

(bottom) A crocodile's teeth interlock and a lower tooth sticks up near its nostrils.

13

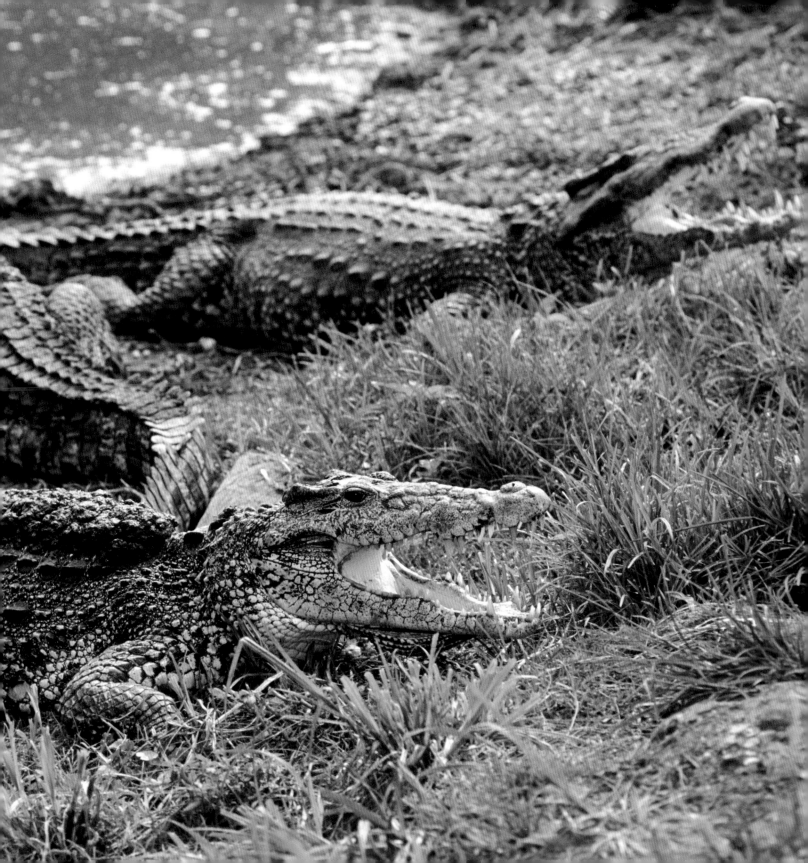

INCREDIBLE SHRINKING WETLANDS

If crocs could describe their ideal home, they'd sum it up in one word: wetlands.

Crocodilians thrive in aquatic habitats or wetlands in tropical and subtropical areas. This can include bodies of water such as ponds, rivers and lakes as well as swamps, lagoons, marshes and bogs. Two species can even survive in saltwater.

Spending time in water is important for several reasons. First, since water doesn't cool or warm up as fast as air, it helps these cold-blooded reptiles keep their body temperatures stable, since they rely on their surroundings for heat. Second, floating in water uses less energy than moving around on land.

But as much as they like water, they couldn't live without land. On cool days they may bask along the shore, using the sun to boost their body heat to ideal levels. On hot days, crocs lie around with their mouths gaping open: they're letting moisture evaporate to help them cool down.

Perhaps most important, crocs lay their eggs on land. Some scrape together vegetation to mound up a nest where eggs mature. Others use sandbanks. Both spots generate heat to help the eggs develop and hatch about two months after being laid.

But the wetlands that crocodilians love are shrinking because of the habits of another creature: humans. When we clear rainforests for logging, more soil is washed into rivers and streams. These waters get shallower and can support fewer fish and other animals that are a croc's food. People in Indonesia have converted hundreds of thousands of acres of mangrove swamps into shrimp farms. In Thailand, mining companies dump their waste into rivers that could be inhabited by crocs. If crocs survive by moving into another area that isn't well suited to their feeding and breeding requirements, then fewer crocs will be born to replace the older ones. Eventually, a whole population could die off.

< On hot days crocs laze around with their mouths open wide: they're letting moisture evaporate to help them cool down.

Imagine spending your family vacation trekking through a South American rainforest looking for brightly colored scarlet macaws perched in hundred-foot (30 m) trees, or trying to spot black caimans, the largest member of the alligator family and one of the forest's many rare and endangered species.

It's taken a long time for people to start thinking of rainforests as valuable enough to protect.

This kind of a holiday—called ecotourism—really exists in the Iwokrama Forest, a lush area of one million acres (371,000 ha) in the heart of Guyana. The Guyanese government started the program to show how tropical forests can be used safely to benefit the local, national and international communities.

Shortly after the program began in 1989, scientists surveyed the black caiman population. They wanted to know how many were left, and where exactly they lived. The caiman's numbers had plunged during the 1960s and 1970s, mainly due to overhunting.

Though black caimans are still prized elsewhere for their shiny skin, at Iwokrama the animals are more valuable if they're lazing on a riverbank. That's because they're a big draw for tourists. At night, guides steer boats along the river and shine lights to spot the red-eyed glare of the black caiman, which can grow more than 13 feet (4 m) long.

Tourist dollars help protect juvenile black caimans on the Iwokrama reserve in Guyana, South America.

It's taken a long time for people to start thinking of rainforests as valuable enough to protect. For years, these areas have been targeted by people and companies who cut down trees for wood, convert the area to farmland or mine precious minerals. What happens when they remove so much from the rainforest that it slowly disappears? Plants and animals lose their habitat, local people have no way of supporting their families, and companies no longer have a place to get the raw materials they need to make money. In short, everybody loses. If Iwokrama goes as planned, companies will still get their resources, people can still carry out their traditional ways of life and the jungle will continue to thrive—everybody wins.

CROCS ON THE ATTACK

∧ Beware: common sense protects against rare croc-human attacks.

It was after dark one night in 1945 when Japanese soldiers serving in World War II were retreating from enemy troops. Near the coast of Burma, they fled through a swamp inhabited by crocodiles. Of the thousand soldiers who trudged through the water that night, only 20 survived.

With chilling stories like this one so widely reported—in fact, it's believed to be a myth—it's no surprise that most people fear crocodilians. But attacks—especially fatal ones—are extremely rare. In Australia's Northern Territory, seven people have been killed by crocodiles in the past 28 years; American gators have killed 14 people in Florida since 1970. The flipside is that humans are the croc's only predator, and we've killed several million of them in the past hundred years.

What is it that makes crocodilians prey on people? Crocs are opportunistic hunters—that means they wait patiently for dinner to come to them, rather than actively seeking it out. This lazy-sounding habit is an incredibly efficient one. Other large predators, such as tigers, use loads of energy roaming around looking for food. By waiting for delivery instead of running for take-out, crocs use much less energy, so they don't need to eat as often. The average croc has a meal just once a week. If it has to, an adult can survive for a year or more without eating anything at all.

So crocodilians won't lumber into a village and tackle a person walking down the street. But if that same person were to cool off in a river inhabited by crocs, or crouch by the edge to wash clothes, the animals could attack. While they rarely go after prey as large as humans, crocs will take whatever wanders into their habitat. Males may also attack during the breeding season, when they become extremely territorial and a person or boat could be considered a threat.

These wildebeests don't look impressed by the Nile crocodile's explosive speed and power.

Almost all fatal attacks could have been prevented with common sense. In Florida, for example, many people ignore warning signs that are posted around known gator-infested lakes. They assume that if they don't see alligators basking on the shore, then there aren't any to worry about. This makes them sitting ducks, since these animals rely on surprise when they hunt, and they're used to hiding and waiting. "Vehicles kill thousands of people every year, and yet we love them in spite of their being killers," says Perran Ross, professor of wildlife, ecology and conservation at the University of Florida, and former executive officer of the Crocodile Specialist Group, a worldwide network of 350 experts. "If only we could treat crocs with the same respect."

About 20 years ago, thousands of broad-snouted caimans (*Caiman latirostris*) were dying every year in Argentina when their marshy homes were drying up. Local people who hunted the caimans were finding it more and more difficult to earn a living. The situation was so grim that the species was considered extinct in the province of Santa Fe. Their habitat was disappearing, too, because people turned to cattle ranching—which involved turning wetlands into pasture—to support themselves.

∧ Broad-snouted caiman eggs are taken to a ranch in Santa Fe, Argentina where the young are raised away from predators. Some are released into the wild while others are sold for meat.

These days, the caiman population has recovered so well that Argentina is the only country in the world where this species' skins are allowed to be traded. The secret? Proyecto Yacaré (yacaré is an Indian word for caiman). "At the beginning, I was aiming just to cure sick animals," says veterinarian Alejandro Larriera, director of the project. "But soon I realized that something had to be done about habitat conservation."

Now local people are hired for caiman ranching, and they earn money for every nest they show to Proyecto Yacaré staff. Landowners also earn cash for every egg harvested, so they work to protect nesting areas and encourage female caimans to lay their eggs on their property. Another bonus: illegal hunting has been mostly eliminated because it doesn't earn local people as much money as they can get by cooperating. In fact, Larriera says almost 400 people earn a living off the program.

Revenue from ranching protects wetlands so caimans like this one can live, hunt, mate and reproduce.

The collected eggs are taken to ranches where the young are raised—some are sold for their meat and skins, while others are released into the wild. People can now buy caiman meat in restaurants and leather goods in shops. Every item comes with a brochure explaining that by buying a caiman product, you're helping preserve Argentina's wetlands.

REPTILES ON RUNWAYS

Today, many consider crocodile and alligator skin the ultimate in luxury. But it was first prized for function, not fashion: soldiers in the U.S. Civil War during the 1860s wore footwear crafted from American alligators. As the supply of gators plummeted by the late 1800s, skins were imported from Central America. When those supplies diminished, more skins were brought from Africa and Asia. During the 1950s, five to 10 million hides a year were being traded.

Since people weren't fond of crocodilians, countries didn't do much to keep track of their croc populations. As millions of animals were hunted every year, it didn't take long for the survival of the 15 commercially traded species (others have skins that are too marked, or too difficult to process) to become severely threatened.

Eventually, countries began to restrict trade. Between 1959 and 1970, most African governments passed laws to protect the Nile and dwarf crocs, among others. Colombia, in South America, forbade hunting and selling of various species in certain areas in 1968. The U.S. did the same for the American alligator.

Unfortunately, these efforts weren't enough to stop illegal traders, who smuggled hides to neighboring countries. Others lied that their hides were from unprotected species, or bribed government officials. In 1973, several nations agreed to work together to make sure that trade wouldn't threaten the survival of crocodilians and other animals and plants. Two years later, the Convention on International Trade in Endangered Species (CITES) came into force.

Under the agreement, countries must record all trade in endangered or vulnerable wildlife, which in 1975 included two-thirds of crocodilians. Officials keep track of every step, from the farmer or hunter who skinned the animal, right up to when it gets turned into leather. Not only has this helped stop illegal trading, but many countries have developed programs for monitoring crocs for the first time—a huge step forward in conservation.

< Many conservationists believe farming, ranching and controlled hunting offer the animals and their habitat a good chance of survival.

WORKING WITH "THE ENEMY"

∧ If the government of Paraguay didn't authorize the hunt and sale of these crocodiles, the animals would probably have died from an increasingly dry habitat.

After governments began to work together successfully, conservationists wondered who they might partner with to continue fighting for the long-term survival of crocodiles and alligators. The surprising answer? Their enemies: hunters, traders and fashion designers.

"Traders and conservationists realized that if crocs were extinct we'd both be out of business," says Perran Ross. "Gradually we developed our common interest and worked together."

The conservationists had a radical idea: not less hunting and trade, but more. How about developing a program that would allow hunters to take some crocs while protecting others in the wild? "If you don't cut your lawn, it gets shaggy and messy," says Ross. "If you mow it once a month, it looks smashing. Crocs are easy to manage in a similar way."

Animal rights activists were furious. But those in the industry—from hunters and croc farmers to designers and retailers—were thrilled at the prospect of getting a steady supply of skins. A limited number could be taken from the wild and others from farm-bred animals. And conservationists were delighted at the possibility of replacing slashed populations: a portion of the eggs taken from the wild would be returned when the animals were juveniles and more likely to survive. "How do you save the alligator?" says Ross. "Turn them into handbags. Recycle the funds from each sale into saving their habitat. Essentially, a few sacrifice themselves for the rest."

24

Consumers who buy luxury goods made of legal crocodile leather are supporting conservation efforts.

It sounded crazy, but the plan worked. These days, about two million skins are traded every year and they bring in over US$500 million, with some of the funds going back into conservation, to keep crocodilian populations strong and healthy. When the CSG began in 1971, all 23 species of croc were endangered or threatened. By 1996, that number had dropped to 15. No other group of vertebrate animals has made such a dramatic comeback.

If Hollywood had an award for the best rags-to-riches story, the American alligator would probably win. In Louisiana, the gator has climbed off the endangered list and its precious wetland habitat is being protected. But this story didn't always look like it would have a happy ending.

In the 1960s, hunting had slashed the state's alligator population from well over a million to less than 100,000. It was so bad that gator hunting was banned in 1963. After years of research, the Louisiana government hatched a three-part plan to benefit alligators, hunters, landowners, wetlands and the state.

The program launched in 1972 with an annual hunt. That was followed in 1986 by an egg harvest, while the first captive-raised animals were released to the wild two years later.

The government calculates how many eggs and gators can be safely taken from the wild each year. The eggs are hatched and raised on farms until they are 4 feet (1.2 m) long. Most of these alligators are sold to make luxury leather products.

^ A gator watches as its eggs are collected. The hatchlings will be raised on an alligator farm.

< American alligators and their habitat are no longer at risk in Louisiana thanks to a farming and hunting program that's been imitated around the world.

American alligators raised in captivity grow as well, or better, than wild gators.

Although a female gator may lay 20 to 50 eggs per year, these can be destroyed by floods or high heat, or get eaten by raccoons and other predators. Small hatchlings are also at risk of being preyed upon, sometimes by larger gators. As a result, only about 14 in 100 will survive to be 4 feet long. That's why 14 percent of all farm-raised juvenile gators—who grow much larger than those in the wild—must be returned to the nesting area where they were collected.

Trappers are allowed to take larger animals, whose skins are prized for making bulkier items such as briefcases and furniture, but they have to follow strict rules. For example, hunting is not allowed at night. And the harvest season is only open during September in open water, since that's the time when breeding females prefer to be deep in the marsh with their hatchlings, far away from hunters in boats.

The release program is equally important. Both females and males are returned to the wild. And juveniles are released in smaller ponds instead of open waters favored by hungry adult gators and other predators.

As a result of all this planning, the wild gator population is thriving. Researchers have found farmed gators are just as successful at finding food as wild ones. Captive-raised alligators grow as well as, or better, than wild alligators, and can successfully breed earlier.

Louisiana's current population of about one million gators is almost the same as what it was a hundred years ago, and the habitat is doing as well as the gators. Most of the wetlands where gators thrive are owned by companies that could make money by converting the land to grow crops or encourage development. Yet since the landowners who participate in the program earn money by selling the eggs collected from their property, they maintain their property so gators will continue to live, mate and lay eggs there.

Farmers get eggs to raise and sell. Hunters are able to earn a living. Tanneries, where leather is made, get a steady supply of skins, and retailers earn money from consumers who buy alligator products. It all adds up to a $30-million industry in Louisiana. It's been so successful that the program has been mimicked around the world.

^ The annual hunt in Louisiana: this one's a keeper.

Biologist Ruth Elsey of the Louisiana Department of Wildlife and Fisheries says the only problem now is clearing up the misconception that alligators are still endangered. "There's a bumper sticker down here that says, 'If you want to save an alligator, buy a handbag,' and that's completely true."

Christine Brewton started working with alligators by accident. In the late 1990s, her triathlon group was preparing for its morning swim in a Louisiana lake when some men in a fishing boat warned them they'd seen an alligator. She thought they were joking: she'd grown up in the 1960s, when gators were much less common. Then she spotted a 9-foot (3 m) male nearby.

∧ The more Christine Brewton learned about gators and the programs that nurture their wetlands, the more she wanted to protect them.

For the next month, Brewton followed the hunter who was hired to remove the gator and wrote a story about her experience for the local newspaper. Her next article started as a warning about the danger from gators, but the more she learned—that attacks were rare, and that the gators help maintain wetlands—the more she wanted to help protect the species. Today, she's part of Louisiana's Fur and Alligator Advisory Council.

Brewton has visited more than 550 of the world's finest boutiques from New York to Milan to educate retailers about Louisiana alligator products. She explains the Marsh to Market program, which produces skins while at the same time protecting wild gators and their habitat. She tells retailers about the history of the marsh, how families have been living off the land for generations, and about the beauty and diversity of the wetlands. When people are squeamish about selling an item made with an animal that was once endangered, she explains that the population now tops one million in Louisiana.

Brewton educates salespeople at fine boutiques around the world. Many don't realize that the once-endangered American alligator is now over a million strong.

As well as statistics, Brewton shares her passion. "I try to get salespeople excited about what we're doing so they won't have any reservations about grabbing a $10,000 purse off the shelf and recommending it to a customer."

The way she sees it, as long as people keep buying American alligator products, the animals and their environment will be considered valuable enough to conserve. Sure, agrees Brewton, in a perfect world we'd just protect animals and their habitat, but she doesn't think that's realistic. She believes when people buy an alligator purse, they're investing in a future for the species. "I often see a light bulb go on for people. They say, 'I never thought of it that way.'"

CROCS IN THE KITCHEN

Crocodile and alligator meat is sold all over the world. The good news is it's a way of making sure the rest of the animal isn't wasted when the skin gets used. The bad news is, just as some endangered crocodilians are poached for their skins, their meat may also be sold illegally.

^ People living in central Africa count on crocodile meat as part of their diet.

People living in central African villages count on crocodile meat as part of their diet. In the past, there were smaller populations of hunters who took only what they needed to feed their families. But now there are millions of people living in these forests, and they rely on bushmeat—meat from wild animals—for food.

Bushmeat hunting has also become a business, as hunters sell the meat to people living in cities. Because of its unique characteristics, the dwarf crocodile (*Osteolaemus tetraspis*) is under severe hunting pressure in Africa. It's the smallest crocodilian species (usually less than 6 feet, or 2 meters), one of the least aggressive, and it can be kept alive for a month or more with no food, water or refrigeration, and then sold in a city for more than it would fetch in a rural village.

Beyond their skin and meat, crocodiles are also prized for their oil and fat, which are used for healing. People in Madagascar, for example, use croc oil to treat burns, allergic skin reactions, skin cancer, even coughs and asthma.

Besides their skin and meat, crocs are also prized for the supposed healing properties of their oil and fat.

Using crocs as a source of medication could be seen as another threat to their survival, but Ross sees it differently. He says if we value their healing properties, that could be another reason to preserve the animals. "While there are many examples of proven medicines made from plants, there are few from animals," he says. "How exciting if crocodiles turn out to be the source of valuable new medicines."

How do you create Europe's largest crocodilian zoo when you've got no formal wildlife education and experts tell you it can't be done? You start when you're 10 years old.

Rene Hedegaard, founder of Denmark's Krokodille Zoo, first laid eyes on a live croc at the city zoo in Copenhagen. "The more I found out about these animals, the more my fascination grew." In seventh grade he announced that one day he would open a terrarium to share his passion with others.

In 1989, he bought a spectacled caiman from a pet store and kept it in a huge aquarium at home. He fed it fish and worms as well as rats and small chickens. "It took me a while to get used to how explosive these animals can be," Hedegaard remembers. "It would lie so still, and then when it wanted to do something it moved so fast."

∧ At Krokodille Zoo in Denmark, Rene Hedegaard breeds Chinese (bottom) and American alligators (top).

Next, he wanted to build a larger facility and collect one individual of every crocodilian species. Experts told him it would be impossible, but Hedegaard started working with zoos, crocodile farms and research centers to buy other species. He wanted to support croc conservation by spreading awareness and raising money. In 2000, he fulfilled his dream and opened Krokodille Zoo on Denmark's Falster Island.

Educating people about the role that crocs play in nature is one of Krokodille Zoo's successes. With 25 specially heated enclosures (Denmark is cold!), Hedegaard and a small staff breed and care for 70 crocs from 19 species. "When schoolchildren first come to the zoo, they act very afraid. They have it in their heads that these are killers," says Hedegaard. "Then we show them how small crocodiles are when they're hatchlings. They get to hold the eggs in their hands and learn about their life cycle, which gets them interested."

Rene Hedegaard with his Chinese alligators just before he puts them in hibernation.

The zoo's other achievement is conserving wild crocs. A portion of every ticket sold goes to projects to help Chinese alligators, Philippine crocodiles and black caimans in their native countries.

Hedegaard has become enough of a crocodile expert that other zoos now turn to him for advice and help with breeding, and in 2003 he was invited to become a member of the Crocodile Specialist Group. His next project: he convinced the Danish government to build another zoo just 4 miles (7 km) from his own and it's set to open in 2006. "It will be a place where we can study and learn even more about these amazing animals."

TROUBLE WITH THE NEIGHBORS

There's something bittersweet about successful conservation efforts when it comes to crocodilians. While growing wild populations are considered good news by conservationists, they can lead to greater threats from the people who live nearby. Take the Chinese alligator, for example. It's not hunted and it enjoys full protection under the law. Yet still it's near the top of the endangered species list. Why? Because it lives in conflict with people.

Thousands of acres of habitat have been converted to farmland, and there are just 130 Chinese alligators left in the wild. The problem is, their daily activities are a pain for their human neighbors. They prey on ducks and fish that people could eat. And they burrow into the ground to escape extreme temperatures, which disrupts the irrigation systems farmers use to water their crops. It's not easy for people to care about an animal that makes life difficult.

The Philippine croc has also suffered because of people's destructive fishing techniques. Dynamite, electricity and chemicals are used to catch fish, which depletes the marine food supply and may accidentally kill crocs. It's hard to convince people to stop, because fish supplies are low and it's not easy to catch a meal with more traditional methods.

And then there is poaching. Laws have helped reduce the illegal trade in these animals, but in some countries, such as Thailand (the original home of the critically endangered Siamese crocodile), there is extensive captive breeding on farms. In order to stock these farms with crocs, people often capture wild crocs and sell them for big money to farms. With just a few hundred Siamese crocodiles remaining in the wild, every sale pushes this species closer to extinction.

< A woman touches an alligator that was caught in her backyard in Miami, Florida. When conservation efforts are successful, people and crocs are at greater risk of bumping into each other.

For 20 years, Bhanumathi loved working as a nature educator in India. Then she quit her job with World Wildlife Fund (WWF) and turned her attention to another activity that has captivated her since childhood: puppetry. Now she's combined these two passions to help people learn about crocs and other animals.

> "Even teachers need to learn more about crocs because they are generally afraid of them."

Before she plunged into her PhD studies in puppetry, Bhanumathi often headed to the Madras Crocodile Bank. It was established back in 1976, when the three Indian species (the gharial, mugger crocodile and saltwater crocodile) were seriously endangered due to habitat loss and overhunting. The Bank has successfully bred these animals in captivity for zoos and to return to the wild, and now houses 3,000 crocodilians from 14 species, plus other endangered reptiles. There, Bhanumathi worked to make people less afraid and more concerned about protecting these creatures.

Bhanumathi and her puppets have traveled to remote areas to teach children about wildlife. She set up a puppet theatre at the Croc Bank and trained three unemployed young people to use traditional puppets to tell stories promoting the message that crocs and reptiles play an important role in nature.

Bhanumathi and her puppets teach children about the importance of crocodile conservation.

Bhanumathi also organized weekend nature camps for city children and ran workshops for adults. "Even teachers need to learn more about crocs because they are generally afraid of them," she says. "At Croc Bank we let them handle baby crocs to overcome their fear. I think it's important because they are role models for children."

But she most enjoys working with kids. "They are the future citizens and decision makers. If I can use puppets to change people's attitudes, then I get a great feeling of satisfaction. If children are motivated, we will have a good future."

^ A representative of the Philippine village of Cadsalan presents his community's croc conservation plan to people from other villages and the local government. Making locals proud – and not afraid – of the Philippine crocodile is one goal of the Philippine CROC Project.

Discovering a Philippine crocodile in the Philippines doesn't sound like a big deal, but in 1999 it was huge. The wild population of the world's most endangered croc species had plunged from 1,000 animals in 1982 to just 100 in 1993. Five years later, wildlife experts had given up on its chances of rebounding in the wild and recommended captive breeding. Then a man caught a small crocodile while fishing in a river on the island of Luzon, where crocs were believed to have already died out.

As it turned out, there were more—scientists counted 27 non-hatchlings in 2004, up from 12 four years earlier. And conserving every one of them is the goal of the Philippine Crocodile Rehabilitation, Observance and Conservation (CROC) Project. The CROC team is trying to turn the croc's biggest enemy—people—into its protectors.

As well as the small and shy Philippine croc, the Philippines is also home to the large and aggressive saltwater crocodile. Most people don't understand the difference, and they trap crocs out of fear, for food or just for fun, since rich people keep hatchlings as pets. Given the croc's terrible reputation, it's perhaps not surprising that the local word for crocodile, buwaya, is used as an insult.

Less than 200 Philippine crocs are left in the wild.

CROC is trying to improve the animal's reputation by informing the public. The team spreads the message that the Philippine croc is not dangerous, and that conserving its habitat is also good for people because it gives them cleaner water, more fish, less soil erosion and more water for their crops. They try to make people on Luzon proud that their crocodiles are the last to survive, and aware that it's their responsibility to guard it from extinction. "We've had a lot of success with this approach," says wildlife biologist and CROC team leader Merlijn Van Weerd. "The people here are proud of anything that is Filipino. Having the crocodile here puts their community on the map."

The response has been encouraging. One local government has agreed to protect the croc by setting aside land for a sanctuary, and people from the community are guarding two other protected areas.

Not only do crocodiles benefit, people do, too. "Their livelihood is improved, more sustainable and more croc-friendly, and we win their support for crocodile conservation," says Van Weerd.

THE NEED TO BREED

Using crocodilians wisely is one way to protect them. Another strategy that is even more widely practiced is captive breeding.

There are two approaches to raising crocs in captivity: farming and ranching. Farms breed baby crocs from a collection of captive-bred adults—no animals are taken from the wild. Ranching, on the other hand, involves collecting eggs, hatchlings or adult crocs from the wild and raising them in captivity. Some farms and ranches release a portion of their captive-raised crocs into the wild once the young are big enough. Other crocs are sold for their skins.

^ A group of hungry crocodiles crawl ashore to feast on chunks of meat put out for them at a European alligator farm.

On farms and ranches that are breeding for skins, the animals are usually raised under ideal conditions so they grow quickly and start breeding sooner. The adult crocs are often kept together in pens with a large pool where they mate. Hatchlings are raised separate from grown crocs to ensure the adults don't feed on the young. The reptiles may be fed chickens, fish and, in cases where crocs are being raised for skins, even crocodile meat.

So, do conservationists prefer farming or ranching? The answer is ranching, because it encourages people to value crocodiles for more than just their skins, says Perran Ross. "Egg collection forces you into a position where you have to protect the wild animals and their habitat, because that's where you get your eggs."

A Louisiana farmer watches over captive-bred hatchling alligators as they're released into a pen.   >

ON THE FRONTLINES | CHINESE ALLIGATORS

When zoologist John Thorbjarnarson went to China a few years ago to study the Chinese alligator, he was shocked at what he saw. Less than 130 alligators remained in the wild, and one of the biggest populations consisted of 11 gators in a pond surrounded by farmhouses, rice paddies and a video rental shop.

It's not exactly what you'd expect for one of China's most respected animals. In its home country, the Chinese alligator is a symbol of power and good fortune, long celebrated in art and folklore. The species is well protected by law—you cannot kill an alligator without going to jail. But there is no protection for their habitat.

The problem is space: the marshy land required by these shy 6-foot (2 m) alligators is the same land needed by farmers to cultivate rice and raise ducks to feed the country's enormous human population. The few places where the alligators remain are ponds owned by local farmers, who are allowed to drain the water to irrigate their rice fields.

∧ This pond in China is used by a local farmer to raise ducks and is also home to a small group of endangered Chinese alligators.

China has reproduced more than 10,000 alligators through captive breeding programs. Yet if their habitat is not expanded, those in the wild are expected to disappear in the next 10 years.

Although the alligators are on the brink of extinction in the wild, they are alive and well in captivity. In the late 1980s, Chinese scientists began to breed these rare creatures, and more than 10,000 alligators now live in breeding centers, most at the Anhui Research Center for Chinese Alligator Reproduction in Xuancheng. The alligators are also bred in foreign zoos. A few are sold for meat and a few are exported to other zoos or private collectors, with the money going back into the breeding program.

Although these numbers are encouraging, captive breeding is not perfect. Some are concerned that the health of Chinese alligators may deteriorate because of inbreeding— that is, closely related animals mating with one another. When two alligators with the same mother produce offspring, the young alligator may be born with defects.

Recently, the focus of the breeding program has shifted toward returning alligators to the wild. In April 2003, the center released three healthy alligators into one of the 13 sites where the animals are clustered. Future plans include restoring habitat and renting land for the alligators from local villagers. That way, communities can earn a livelihood from the land, and the animals get a safe place to live.

The last possibility? Selling more alligator meat to local restaurants. In China, the meat is thought to have health benefits, including fending off old age. Making itself useful, says Thorbjarnarson, may increase the Chinese alligator's chances of surviving.

< Conservationist John Thorbjarnarson and Ding Youzhong release a juvenile alligator into a protected site in China's Anhui province.

RISKY REPRODUCTION

Captive breeding was once cheered as a conservation solution. Some believed that if crocodilians could be bred in captivity, people would leave the wild ones alone. But in a few places where there's extensive captive breeding—including China—the wild population has diminished. "Once people feel secure about what's happening in captivity, they ignore the pressures on the wild population and their habitat," says Perran Ross. In Thailand, where captive breeding is very popular, highly endangered Siamese crocs are no longer hunted for skins. Now, they're trapped in the wild and sold to breeders.

∧ In the wild, croc eggs provide food for other animals such as this Monitor lizard.

Captive breeding has other drawbacks. Sometimes, two different kinds of croc mate together on a farm to create a hybrid—an animal that's a mix of two species. Farmers in Thailand, for example, breed their native Siamese crocodiles with saltwater crocodiles in order to produce a higher-quality skin faster. If one of these hybrids goes to another farm or into the wild, it could mate with pure breeds and produce more unnatural hybrids. Even when there is no mixing of species, the crocs may be in danger of serious health problems because of inbreeding.

Nor can animals living in pens do all the things crocs do for the environment. In the wild, crocs are at the top of the food chain, so they keep prey species in check by feeding on them, provide food for others that prey on their eggs and young, and enrich the water and marine life through nutrients in their waste.

Captive breeding isn't a perfect conservation solution. In Thailand, some farmers breed Siamese crocs with saltwater crocs to produce a higher quality skin faster. These hybrids could change wild populations.

Finally, even if a program is successful at breeding a species in captivity, it's often difficult to find suitable habitat to release them into. Which is why the best projects take a two-part approach, combining both breeding and habitat protection or restoration.

When Yosapong Temsiripong discovered there were just 10 wild Siamese crocodiles remaining in Thailand, he was moved do something about it. After all, he grew up on his family's crocodile farm. "I realized that if something happened to our farmed crocs, we'd have no more to get from the wild. From that day, I started to learn more about how to use crocs sustainably." His dream: to introduce captive-bred crocs into the wild.

In the mid-1900s, the wild population plummeted from overhunting, but the industry still needed skins, so crocodile farms sprang up to meet demand. Instead of killing them, hunters now trapped wild crocs to sell to farms, which need adult males and females for breeding.

To learn more about the plight of crocs, Temsiripong traveled across the world to the University of Florida, where he became a herpetologist—a scientist who studies reptiles and amphibians. He returned home to manage the family business and soon joined the Crocodile Management Association of Thailand, where he's helping research the introduction of captive-bred Siamese crocs into the wild.

One of his challenges is finding them a home. Ideally, he'd like to let the crocs go in a suitable habitat where wild crocs already live. The location should also be remote, to make it harder for poachers. But tracking down the remaining Siamese crocs won't be easy: a few sightings have been reported in an isolated national park accessible only by boat and on foot through steep and rugged terrain.

Temsiripong also needs to identify purebred Siamese crocodiles on farms—releasing a hybrid could be devastating, since it could breed with real Siamese crocs and dilute the remaining population. To identify the purebreds, he plans to compare DNA samples from farm crocs with samples from a wild population.

The young scientist faces many obstacles, but he's optimistic. "Crocs are my family business, my friends and my future. I know I am moving in the right direction."

Introducing Siamese crocs into the wild is a dream for Yosapong Temsiripong, who grew up on his family's > croc farm in Thailand.

TURN DOWN THE HEAT

In 2004, scientists made a frightening prediction: at least a quarter of the world's land animals and plants—more than one million species—could be wiped out if global warming continues over the next 50 years.

The problem with rising temperatures—even as little as one degree warmer than average—is they cause rising water levels. This means some areas would gradually become flooded, drowning plants and leaving animals without a place to live.

∧ Rising water levels, due to global warming, may threaten animals such as this female Nile crocodile, who needs land to build a nest and lay eggs.

Since gators and crocs spend much of their lives in the water, rising levels aren't such a big deal, right? Wrong. These reptiles are strong swimmers, but females need land to build nests and lay eggs. And crocs and gators also need a shoreline for basking, which helps them keep their body temperature normal.

So what does global warming mean to crocodilians? Some wildlife experts point out that alligators and crocodiles roamed with the dinosaurs: if they survived whatever wiped out those mighty beasts, surely they can handle global warming. Others are less optimistic. They say that if warming continues at the current rate, many wetlands near the coast are doomed. Some species, such as the rare Cuban crocodile, could lose their entire habitat.

If global warming continues, experts predict the coastal wetlands of the Cuban crocodile could be wiped out.

Lots can be done to prevent these disasters, and you don't need to be a wildlife expert. Governments can pass laws that reduce air pollution, since global warming is caused by certain gases in the atmosphere. People can do their part by driving cars less, and cycling, walking or riding buses and subways more. Not only are these changes good for animals and plants, they make the air cleaner for all of us.

AT WORK | LOUIS GUILLETTE

American Louis Guillette was a 9-year-old boy watching underwater explorer Jacques Cousteau on TV when he first announced that he wanted to be a biologist. He was fascinated with the idea of working with animals—especially alligators. "I'm one of those adults who never grew up," says Guillette, a zoology professor at the University of Florida. "I was always interested in dinosaurs, and when I'm studying gators and crocs, I feel like I'm getting to learn about dinosaurs." He even worked as a consultant for the movie *Jurassic Park*.

But you're more likely to find Guillette working in the field than on movie sets. He regularly heads out with a few students in an airboat—a special boat that slides on top of the water so as not to harm anything below the surface. They work at night, because alligators are nocturnal. To find them, they use high-powered flashlights: when the beam hits a gator, its eyes shine a reddish-orange colour.

To catch the animals, they often use nothing more than bare hands. While one person drives the boat into position, Guillette (or one of his students) leans over, grabs the gator behind the head and rolls it back into the boat, holding it on his lap for inspection. To keep those powerful jaws shut, he uses decidedly low-tech tools: thick rubber bands from an office supply store, or good old duct tape. Then he closes the animal's eyes to help it relax while he checks it over. The team also takes a blood and urine sample. If an animal is more than six feet (2 m) long, they catch it using a long pole with a kind of lasso on it.

What is Guillette looking for? He's interested in how pollutants affect alligators and their habitat. He's discovered that pesticides can affect hormone levels and reproduction in alligators. Even when lakes are relatively clean, pesticides can seep into the food chain. That means gators can pick up contaminants by eating the fish, and females then deposit the chemicals in their eggs, causing birth defects.

Taking a gator's blood sample is easier at night, says zoology professor Louis Guillette, since the animals are nocturnal.

Scientists are worried that Guillette's findings show that hazardous levels of pollution have become a regular part of the environment, at least in Florida. Their future could be in danger since their ability to give birth to healthy offspring appears to be at risk. "They are a keystone species. They live a long time and they're near the top of the food chain," says Guillette. "So if they're unhealthy, it tells us the whole lake is unhealthy, including the fish and birds."

In September 2004, Guillette started working with colleagues in Africa to find out whether Nile crocodiles are showing similar defects and abnormalities from pollution in the water—the same water that millions of people drink every day. "These animals are sentinels for our health and the health of our kids," believes Guillette. "We need to know what's making them sick, not only to protect them, but to push for clean drinking water to protect ourselves."

WHAT IS THE CROC'S FUTURE?

In some parts of the world, crocodilians are thriving. In others, they're barely surviving. The American alligator is used extensively for its skin, yet its population is more than two million strong, thanks to careful programs that have since been copied to help other endangered crocs. Success stories like this make many experts optimistic about the future for some crocodilians.

Some, but not all. The Chinese alligator is not hunted, not used for leather and it lives in specially protected reserves. Yet there are just 130 in the wild. Stories like this encourage conservationists to continue their work so that no crocodilian becomes extinct.

Fortunately, the wildlife biologists, herpetologists and conservationists—and even traders and fashion designers—are a creative group. They've found surprising ways to protect species by encouraging the trade in croc skins, even after some people said the idea was crazy.

Making people aware of the importance and value of crocs will always be key. And so will protecting and restoring wetland habitats. The more people can benefit from the well-being of crocodilians, the more likely they'll support conservation. But without ensuring that crocs have a suitable place to live in the wild, it's difficult to help endangered populations recover.

Remember, crocs roamed with the dinosaurs. With research and the dedication of experts, they have a good chance of surviving the next 240 million years.

< The survival of crocodilians depends on making people aware of their importance and value, as well as protecting and restoring their wetland habitats.

FAST FACTS

Scientific names • there are 23 species of crocodilian, making up three families in the reptile order Crocodylia: crocodiles, dwarf crocs and false gharials; alligators and caimans; and gharials.

Size • length from snout to tail ranges from 4 feet (1.2 m) in small females up to 23 feet (7 m) in large males.

• weight about 100 pounds (45 kg) in small females to over 2,200 pounds (1,000 kg) in large males

Life span • 40 to 50 years in the wild (60+ in captivity)

• one croc in a Russian zoo was reportedly 115 when he died in 1997

Locomotion • three ways of moving on land: the belly crawl, with legs out to each side and tummy low, almost like a lizard; the high walk, with limbs under the body instead of out to the sides; and the gallop, a quick movement that smaller species use to escape from danger

• crocs prefer to swim, using their strong tails to propel them

• can explode several feet out of the water to lunge toward prey; when attacking, they can move up to 17 mph (27 kph) for short bursts

Senses and Communication • sensory cells appear as tiny spots on the skin; they may help crocs detect prey and sense changes in the salt content of water

• poor underwater vision, but good binocular vision on land—both eyes work together to figure out distance

• communicate with sounds, postures, motions, odors and by touch

• use more sounds than any other reptile, including grunts, hisses or coughs to scare off threats and bellows to communicate during mating season

Feeding
- can survive underwater without taking a breath for 30+ minutes, though most dives last 10 to 15 minutes
- crocs often drown land mammals, but do not eat their prey underwater or they'd swallow too much fluid
- have many teeth (60 to 110) but can't chew; use jaws to crush prey
- rip apart large prey by whipping the head around or twisting the body until a chunk is torn off
- swallows by flipping back its head so the food is tossed toward the back of the mouth
- large adults may survive a year or more without food

Reproduction
- courtship and mating usually occurs in spring and summer
- a clutch of eggs (30 to 50 on average) is laid during the summer
- females lay eggs in nests made of mounds of mud and vegetation or holes dug in the sand
- eggs take about 90 days to hatch
- sex of crocodilian eggs is determined by the temperature in the nest: high temperatures produce males, low temperatures yield females; both sexes are produced at moderate temperatures

Social life
- males are territorial
- more attentive to their young than any other reptile; adults may gently crack open eggs and carry hatchlings to the water
- hatchlings stay close to parents for up to two years; one female may take over maternal duties for hatchlings from other parents

HOW YOU CAN HELP

If you're interested in learning more about alligators and crocodiles or the projects designed to protect them, contact one of the following organizations or visit their websites:

Crocodile Specialist Group
www.flmnh.ufl.edu/
herpetology/crocs.htm

Box 530, Sanderson NT, 0812, Australia
A worldwide network of experts working on a variety of projects to protect crocodilians. Check out their photo gallery.

Crocodilians: Natural History and Conservation
www.crocodilian.com

Information on all 23 species, plus croc sounds, a question-and-answer section and a detailed guide to keeping crocs as pets.

World Conservation Society
www.wcs.org

2300 Southern Boulevard, Bronx, NY, U.S.A. 10460
Phone (718) 220-5100
Discover efforts to conserve the world's five most endangered crocs.

Animal Planet: Ferocious Crocs
www.animal.discovery.com/
convergence/safari/crocs/
crocs.html

Information on crocodiles, including a photo gallery, quizzes, and answers to your croc questions from an expert.

Crocodile Library
www.tiho-hannover.de/croc

A collection of articles and publications on crocodiles.

Crocodilian Photo Gallery
*www.flmnh.ufl.edu/natsci/
herpetology/crocs/
Crocpics.htm*

A collection of photographs of alligators, crocodiles, caimans and gharials.

The Gator Hole
*http://home.cfl.rr.com/
gatorhole/*

Information on American alligators, including habitat, feeding and mating habits.

Krokodille Zoo
www.krokodillezoo.dk

Europe's largest collection of crocodilians.

Madras Crocodile Bank
www.madrascrocodilebank.org

Located in India, this center helps conserve crocs and other reptiles.

**Michigan Museum of
Zoology's Animal Diversity
Website**
*http://animaldiversity.ummz.
umich.edu/chordata/reptilia/
crocodilia.html*

Information on crocodiles, including a photo gallery and bone specimens.

INDEX

PHOTO CREDITS

AUTHOR'S NOTE

This book is dedicated to my family. Thanks to Morgan for her pick-me-up smiles, to Rylie for his inspiring croc storybook, and to Rob for encouraging me with a steady tide of love and popcorn.

I am particularly grateful to Dr. Perran Ross, former executive officer of the Crocodile Specialist Group (CSG), for being generous with his time and expertise.

Writing this book has given me the privilege of interviewing talented scientists, conservationists, wildlife biologists and herpetologists in Argentina, Australia, Cambodia, Denmark, Guyana, India, Philippines, Thailand and the United States. Thanks to Bhanumathi, Christine Brewton, Adam Britton, Jenny Daltry, Ruth Elsey, Louis J. Guillette Jr., Rene Hedegaard, Alejandro Larriera, Yosapong Temsiripong, John Thorbjarnarson, Merlijn Van Weerd and Graham Watkins.